CW01091589

Russian Tortoise a

Handbook for Beginners:

Detailed Guide on How to

Effectively Raise Russian Tortoise

as Pets & Other Purposes;

Includes Its Care& Diseases;

Feeding; Choosing a Breed; Its

Home & So On

By

Markus J. Muench

Copyright@2020

TABLE OF CONTENTS

CHAPTER ONE

INTRODUCTION

.

Russian turtles (Testudohorsefieldi) are superb little turtles with enormous attributes or characters. Extending in size from 5 to 8 inches in length and weighing about a half pound to over two pounds (300 to 1500 gms), they can be kept outside in Arizona or can regularly do very well with generally unassuming indoor confining.

Shockingly the majorities of the Russian turtles are wild-gotten creatures and are worried when they are gotten back. It is normal for recently bought turtles to have different parasites, herpesviruses, upper respiratory contaminations, and different issues. Conversely, hostage reared infants are solid and once in a while create issues if their cultivation is acceptable.

Besides, Russian turtles do well in fitting open air fenced in areas in the Valley of

the Sun. They may remain outside all
year with suitable consideration
regarding giving a decent resting spot
and keeping out predators and rodents.

**Assortments as well as Natural
Habitat**

Likewise called the Horse field's Tortoise,
the Afghan, the focal Asian, the Steppe,
or the four-toed turtle, these creatures
are found in rough deserts in Russia,
Iran, Pakistan, as well as Afghanistan,
regularly at exceptionally high heights.
There, they live in huge underground

tunnels, where they rest for a long time during seasons of limits in temperature.

These turtles are ordinarily caught in the wild and brought into the U.S. for the homegrown pet exchange. They are additionally reproduced in little numbers in the U.S. furthermore, can be found available to be purchased in pet stores. A few might be found, as well, for reception from salvage associations over the U.S.

Russian Tortoise Care Level

With a moderately little size however large character, the Russian Tortoise is one of the most famous turtles kept as a pet. They are exceptionally dynamic and receptive to their proprietors, and they make incredible first reptiles when thought about appropriately.

They are generally simple to think about, comparative with certain other reptile species, and have genuinely long life expectancies, frequently living for over 40 years.

Russian Tortoise Size as well as Its Appearance

Conceived at about an inch long, these turtles may arrive at 8-10 inches-in length when they are experienced, with females being somewhat bigger than guys.

The Russian Tortoise's carapace (top aspect of the shell) ranges from a tan to yellow to olive shading, with earthy colored to dark markings. The plastron (base shell) is either strong dark or has blotches of earthy colored or dark. Their tail tip is hard and hard and longer in guys, and their skin is tan to yellow hued. One remarkable component that makes Russian Tortoises stand apart from different turtles is the presence of four hooks on each foot – subsequently, their other known name, the four-*toed tortoise.*

Russian Tortoise Meals or Diets

Russian Tortoises are herbivores (plant eaters). They love to eat and by and large incline toward verdant greens. Preferably, they ought to devour a high fiber diet of roughage, dull lettuces, and greens, for example, collards, kale, and turnip, mustard, and dandelion greens, alongside different vegetables, including squash, corn, peppers, carrots, thorny pear prickly plant, and yams. They likewise can have a modest quantity of organic product, for example, apples and berries. Russian Tortoises ought not be taken care of supplement insufficient ice sheet lettuce, grains, or meat.

While financially accessible pelleted consumes less calories exist for Russian Tortoises, a significant number of them contain abundance levels of starch and are not healthfully adjusted. Despite the fact that conclusions on supplementation contrast, a changed vegetable-based eating regimen enhanced with a light cleaning of calcium powder containing nutrient D3 two times per week is ideal, particularly in the event that they are housed inside with restricted UV light introduction, or in the event that they are developing or pregnant.

Grown-up, non-rearing turtles housed outside with full UV introduction and took care of a differed diet for the most part needn't bother with normal calcium or nutrient supplementation.

Turtles ought to be furnished with water in shallow dishes in which they can drench to remain hydrated and which ought to be changed day by day. Turtles regularly poop in their water bowls when they splash; accordingly, it might be smarter to drench pet turtles outside of their nooks a couple of times each week for 30 minutes to forestall changing their drinking water more than once every day. Child turtles specifically experience the ill effects of drying out at high temperatures and ought to be splashed three times each week in a shallow skillet of warm water.

And Russian tortoise can cost up to $214 or $299 or a little less than the amount; however, the price may vary from place to place.

The next chapters will reveal all you need to know regarding your Russian tortoise from *a to z; care, feeding, housing, diseases and remedies; how to sex it and lots more.*

CHAPTER TWO

FUNDAMENTAL CARE, HOUSING REQUIREMENT, DIETS & REQUIRED ENVIRONMENT OF RUSSIAN TORTOISE

You need a pen around 4 feet in length by 4 feet wide to keep a solitary Russian turtle and about twofold that space in the event that you plan on keeping two. It is significant that this space has shade to shield them from the blasting summer sun and splendid bright regions during the cooler months. Shade can be given by local plants like PaloVerde trees, desert willow, jojoba hedges, desert savvy, weak brambles, and thorny pear. Colorful plants like citrus trees are extraordinary shade suppliers however since they don't drop their leaves as the seasons change they may hinder a lot of sun throughout the winter. Russian turtles need a protected retreat wherein they can rest when the temperatures are excessively cold for movement. In a perfect world, a

Russian turtle yard ought to be sufficiently huge to oblige two separate counterfeit tunnels, a midyear one that opens with a northern to eastern presentation and a winter one that opens to a southern introduction. The counterfeit tunnel openings should be raised or in any case ensured with the goal that weighty winter or summer downpours don't flood the tunnel. In the event that you can't give a decent winter nook in your yard, your Russian turtle should sleep inside in a fake hibernaculum.

The walled in area ought to be rich with grasses, spurges, and other reasonable plants for eating. Bermuda, rye, and fescue grass might be planted to give grasses consistently. A few types of grass local to North America are accessible through online seed indexes. Wild weeds are regularly promptly devoured albeit some might be poisonous. Other appropriate peruse plants are hibiscus hedges (leaves and blossoms are promptly eaten) and mulberry trees (leaves and berries). With a suitable lavishly planted walled in area, supplemental taking care of with produce is limited. In any case, a blend of romaine lettuce, green or red leaf lettuce, escarole, kale, collard greens, mustard greens, turnip greens, spinach, broccoli, and other dull green verdant vegetables might be offered to protect that a turtle has enough food. Littler turtles may require day by day plates of mixed greens while grown-ups by and large excel on a few servings of mixed greens seven days, notwithstanding their every day touching. Over-taking care of produce, or offering produce that is high in straightforward sugars and dampness, for example, bananas and apples, may prompt the runs. Sprinkling calcium, for example, calcium carbonate, calcium lactate, or calcium citrate, onto the plate of mixed greens will help balance out the mineral substance of the food. In the event that a turtle approaches earth, it appears to not require minor elements added to the produce. Infrequently supplementation with a legitimate multivitamin might be advantageous. Be certain the nutrient is new—most powdered nutrients lose their strength inside a half year of tearing open the seal, and they lose it all the more rapidly whenever presented to mugginess and temperatures above 78°F for any time allotment.

When in doubt a male Russian turtle won't endure another male in a similar nook. It might likewise badger a female endless reproducers end up just saving the male with the female for brief timeframes during the rearing season. We don't suggest that you house two Russian male turtles together since almost certainly, the least prevailing one will wind up harmed, flipped on his back in the blistering sun, or constantly focused and vulnerable to infection. Females are normally open minded toward one another however some can become menaces and cause the subordinate females to shroud a great deal and become debilitated from pressure. On the off chance that you do attempt to keep groups of Russian turtles, give a lot of concealing spaces and loads of plants and logs to separate the sight lines so they can undoubtedly escape one another.

An open air fenced in area of at any rate 4 ft by 4 ft will easily house a solitary grown-up Russian turtle while a 8 ft by 4 ft nook can house a male and a female, a male and two females, or a few grown-up female turtles. A bigger nook gives more assortments in landscape to the turtles to investigate. Shape the scene so there are a lot of visual hindrances that permit the turtles to avoid each other's sight lines in the event that they so want.

A cinderblock divider at any rate two feet high is a great border fence for a Russian turtle walled in area however you may must have a lip that ventures around 4 creeps into the nook as they can climb shockingly well. The balance should be in any event 12 inches down with the goal that the turtle cannot burrow, underneath the divider. On the off chance that the fence is strong, the turtle won't attempt to get away. Be that as it may, if a turtle can see through the fence, it will zero in on those holes and battle to leave. This can bring about wounds so we don't suggest wire, equipment material, steel, or woven wooden wall.

Standing water may prompt the spread of illnesses, for example, Hexamita and other protozoan parasites. We accept that transitory water, for example, a skillet that is occupied a couple of times each week and left dry on different days, is the most ideal approach to give water to grown-up Russian turtles. A week after week early daytime sprinkling of the yard will likewise offer your Russian turtle a chance to drink. A clock can be set up to occasionally water various areas of the nook and give diverse drinking spots. Keep in mind, turtles are frequently up and moving before breakfast throughout the late spring months so you ought to give new water promptly in the day during the most smoking climate.

Fake tunnels can be developed without any problem. We trust it is imperative to fabricate tunnels with simple admittance to the inside so sleeping turtles might be occasionally observed. A midyear tunnel gives a retreat from the most sizzling daytime temperatures. Confronting the tunnel so it opens in a northerly to easterly course is ideal. With an eastern presentation, the turtle will be awoken by early morning sun and begin movement early, resigning mid-morning to dodge the burning evening beams. It is useful to gently fog tunnels during sweltering climate with the goal that they additionally fill in as a region of higher mugginess than their environmental factors. A winter tunnel gives stable temperatures during the coldest long stretches of winter, keeping the turtle well above freezing all through hibernation. Confronting south is significant with the goal that the winter tunnel gets a lot of sun on the splendid hotter long stretches of fall, winter, and spring.

CHAPTER THREE

TH E CLEAR DISTINCTION BETWEEN A SULCATA TORTOISE &A RUSSIAN TURTLE, PLUS HOW TO EFFECTIVELY SEX A RUSSIAN TORTIOSE

At the point when you are searching for a pet that doesn't shed, the turtle is one to consider. Sulcata turtles and Russian turtles are two famous yet very various choices. Despite the fact that these pets are generally low-support, they require an appropriate environment and quality food and care. Before choosing which one to get back, consider their disparities to figure out which species best accommodates your conditions.

Causes

Sulcata turtles started in the hot, dry atmosphere of Northern Africa and are local to nations, for example, Senegal, Niger and Ethiopia. These turtles advanced to use water productively to make due in dry atmosphere and burrow tunnels to get away from the warmth. They live in parched environments extending from the sandy steppes to dry and rough slopes.

Its Size

Sulcata turtles are a lot bigger than Russian turtles. The third biggest turtle species, sulcatas might be 24 to 30 inches in length and 80 to 110 pounds. Russian turtles are a lot littler, guys estimating just 6 to 8 inches in length. Females are somewhat bigger, growing 8 to 10 creeps long.

Hibernation

Sulcata turtles don't rest; in imprisonment they should have a warm, dry condition all year. Preferably, evening time temperature ought to be during the 70s Fahrenheit. On the off chance that you live in a cold or wet condition, make certain to give an indoor nook to permit the turtle to remain warm. Wild Russian turtles sleep as long as nine months every year. They don't have to rest in bondage if their fenced in area is kept warm. Numerous proprietors, particularly those living in colder atmospheres, decide to sleep their turtles by setting them in a cool nook, in a perfect world 39 to 41 degrees Fahrenheit.

Lodging and Temperature

Sulcata turtles must have a huge nook for meandering around. Because of their enormous size, indoor lodging isn't suggested for grown-up sulcatas. The temperature in the living space ought to be somewhere in the range of 85 and 105 degrees Fahrenheit during the day and into the 70s around evening time. Sulcatas don't swim, so give water in a shallow tub. Russian turtles are all the more handily kept inside because of their littler size, however they actually need an enormous walled in area to move around in. Whenever kept outside, their walled in area must be protected from predators, for example, raccoons. Russian turtles dwell in cooler temperatures than their sulcata counterparts. Ideal daytime temperature ought to be somewhere in

the range of 70 and 80 degrees
Fahrenheit, evening time temperatures
60 to 65 degrees. Give your turtle a
lounging zone at roughly 95 degrees.

The Most Effective Method to Sex Your Tortoise

Grown-up Russian turtles are anything
but difficult to sex. Normally they must
be around 4 inches some time before it's
a slam dunk to tell just by looking. For
individuals who just can hardly wait, we
can sex adolescent turtles utilizing
endoscopy to glimpse inside and see
whether they have ovaries or testicles.

Tail of a male Russian turtle. There is a "spike" (a little scope) at the tip of the tail and the cloaca (or vent) is put at the tip of the tail. A female has an a lot shorter tail, no spike, and the cloaca is a lot nearer to the plastron (lower shell).

Another perspective on a male Russian turtle's tail. Note the spike at the tip of the tail. The tail bends around to contact the upper leg and is any longer than a female's.

CHAPTER FOUR

RUSSIAN TORTOISE AILMENTS/ ILLNESSES & THE DEVICES YOU NEED TO KEEP IT

Russian turtles (Testudo or Agrionemyshorsfieldii) are boundless in the realm of pet reptiles. These smallish turtles, as their names express, hail from Russia, yet in addition from China, Azerbaijan, Pakistan, Turkmenistan, Iran, Armenia and Oman. They are likewise regularly alluded to as both "Afghan turtles" as well as "steppe turtles."

Russian Tortoise Common Illnesses Plus Signs of Health

Some clinical sicknesses are moderately ordinary in Russian turtles, so it is essential to stay cautious with respect to their wellbeing. These conditions incorporate skin parasites, for example, bugs, stomach related issues, breathing issues and bone issues. On the off chance that a Russian turtle is sound and liberated from squeezing wellbeing concerns, he ought to have a solid appearance, too. Consistently look at your pet for signs of solid wellbeing, some of which remember eating for a normal premise, ready eyes with no murkiness or shadiness, a spotless nose territory, a lot of physical development and nonattendance of anomalies on both the skin and the shell. Regardless of whether your turtle has all the earmarks of being liberated from disease, notwithstanding, that may not be the situation.

Reasons for Breathing Problems

Breathing issues incidentally emerge in pet Russian turtles. These issues may happen because of natural elements, to be specific stretched out introduction to over the top wetness and cool temperatures. For Russian turtles, cool temperatures are commonly just sensible when the air is dry. A few indications of respiratory conditions in Russian turtles remember both nasal release and trouble for breathing typically.

Dietary Deficiencies

Dietary inadequacies are additionally now and then an issue for Russian turtles, frequently because of absence of bright B (UVB) introduction in their living spaces.

Veterinarian Appointments as well as Signs of Illness

It is essential to get your pet Russian turtle for customary outlandish vet tests, even just after you initially get him. Parasites are a typical illness in these small reptiles, so ensure that a vet arrangement is the main thing on your rundown once you settle on the choice to take one of these pets in. After your turtle's underlying visit, take him to the vet for yearly tests. On the off chance that you actually notice indications of disease, nonetheless, prompt vet care is an absolute necessity. A few signs of discomfort are weariness, free stools, hunger misfortune, wheezing and abnormal blotting on either the skin or the shell. With the correct consideration and veterinary consideration, pet Russian turtles can frequently outperform 40 years in age.

What unit do I requirement for a turtle?

Notwithstanding their strong shell and amazing future, turtles are fragile animals that require a considerable measure of care under quite certain conditions.

To keep a turtle you will require a:

-Turtle table

-Cleaned soil

-UVB light

-Turtle run

-Warmth relaxing light

-Darkening indoor regulator

-Earthenware heat producer

-Heartbeat indoor regulator

-Turtle food

-Turtle pet protection

-Turtle vet

Having a broad turtle pack is
fundamental for your misdeed's
prosperity.

CHAPTER FIVE

MORE DETAILS ABOUT THE CARE OF A RUSSIAN TORTOISE

On the off chance that there is any uncertainty that there is acceptable waste in a region throughout the late spring storms or the winter downpours, you should assemble a hill of earth up to 12 inches high where you need to find the tunnel. The structure might be a cinderblock square with a pressed wood rooftop secured with a thick layer of protecting soil. Parcels of straw can be masterminded along these lines, however for the most part should be supplanted each year. Huge trash bins half-covered in the ground are utilized effectively by a few.

Some Russian turtles will unearth their own tunnels instead of utilization the fake tunnels that have been given. This ought to be debilitated in light of the fact that it very well may be hard to screen the strength of a turtle in a characteristic tunnel.

The outside fenced in area for hatchlings and turtles under 4 inches in length: Basically, the nooks for hatchling and adolescent turtles are equivalent to the walled in areas for grown-ups just with the fake tunnels custom fitted to their littler sizes. The fake tunnels ought to be clouded all the more frequently to keep up the higher stickiness that youthful Russian turtles need. Water should be accessible day by day and an absorbing warm water each week will safeguard that the little desert turtle remains very much hydrated. Work mesh might be set over the head of the turtle walled in area to keep meandering felines and different predators from pestering the children.

Since little Russian turtles can rapidly capitulate to subterranean insect nibbles, it is essential to altogether scour the nook each 3 or 4 days for creating subterranean insect hills and to wipe out those when found. A wire hindrance can be set over the bedeviled ant colony to forestall the child turtles from expending the Amdro.

A grown-up turtle will regularly well in an indoor pen that is around 6 ft by 2 ft and littler turtles might be housed in littler nooks. Round walled in areas, (for example, round steer's troughs) give more region to wander than the "curved" troughs, however are frequently hard to move through passages and fit into little rooms. Hatchlings may live easily in a 20 gallon long aquarium, or a walled in area 24 to 30 inches in length and 12 to 18 inches wide.

Distinctive turtle attendants depend on various substrates. We accept old fashioned Arizona soil is a phenomenal substrate for Russian turtles however may make the degree of residue in your home agonizing. The earth must be gathered from a region that isn't debased with pesticides, herbicides, engine oil, or other harmful substances, and isn't polluted with parasites or ailments from different turtles. Cypress mulch functions admirably for most circumstances where soil isn't viable. Bunny pellets, either packed timothy roughage or hay feed, are regularly utilized with little turtles. Care must be taken to spot clean it every day and to totally change the substance out at any rate once per month to maintain a strategic distance from shape development on these pellets. Turtles will excel on paper towels or papers for brief timeframes as might be suggested following a medical procedure or different disease.

A slip-up numerous individuals make is to expect a Russian turtle needn't bother with water. Actually, Russian turtles in the wild search out tunnels that have a higher stickiness than the encompassing ground surface. At the point when kept inside, a basic "stickiness box" comprises of a little encased plastic compartment, similar to a Rubbermaid sweater box, loaded up with moist sphagnum greenery and a little entryway cut in the side. The turtle can carry to and fro among damp and dry territories varying. The greenery should be changed normally and should be kept marginally clammy instead of sopping wet. A decent adjudicator of wetness is to attempt to press water out of the clammy greenery. On the off chance that you can just get a drop or two; the greenery is the perfect measure of wet. While grown-up turtles may do totally well without a moistness box during their time inside, youthful developing turtles may experience the ill effects of a shell deformation known as pyramiding in the event that they don't approach higher dampness consistently.

A shallow water dish should be accessible around three times each week. Likewise with the open air turtles, standing water that has been dirtied by the turtle appears to advance certain intestinal parasites. We would say, faucet water is a satisfactory wellspring of consumable water, yet a few guardians like to utilize sifted or filtered water. Turn around assimilation or refined water ought not to be utilized as it is totally ailing in minerals.

You can't repeat all the characteristics of normal daylight with lights. All things considered, turtles might be effectively held under counterfeit lighting long haul. Bright B must be given by one of the bulbs to help in calcium digestion and other significant physiological cycles. There are various brands of bulbs that guarantee to give this, yet the vast majority of our encounters have been with Reptisun and Power sun bulbs. These ought to be on for 8-12 hours every day. Brilliant white light is expected to counterbalance the somewhat blue light gave by the bright creating bulbs. This white light permits more genuine hues— that it, the hues show up more as they do under the sun—which is imperative to animate taking care of conduct and different exercises in numerous turtles. The brilliant white light ought to be on 8 hrs per day throughout the winter and 14 hrs every day during the pinnacle of the late spring. A third light source ought to give warm luxuriating territories, where the temperatures arrive at 95°F during the center of the day. By and large a blend of bright light bulbs, brilliant bulbs, and a mercury fume light might be expected to give the nature of light expected to keep Russian turtles solid inside. The photoperiod ought to continuously change consistently despite the fact that turtles that are by and large deliberately "kept conscious" through hibernation should remain on a 12 hr on, 12 hr off photoperiod.

It is essential to have cool and warm zones all through the nook so a turtle can control its internal heat level. The foundation temperature during the day ought to be 85-88°F with an evening drop to around 75-80°F. In the event that a turtle is sick, the temperature ought to never dip under 82-85°F around evening time. A brilliant lounging light ought to give a zone where the temperature is 95-100°F during the day. While glowing spot lights are extraordinary wellsprings of warmth during the day, and red-colored bulbs can be utilized for evening time heat sources, in many cases brilliant warmth boards give all the more in any event, warming all through an encased space. The brilliant warmers discharge no noticeable light, in contrast to red bulbs, and don't interfere with a turtle's sleep. It is essential to have an indoor regulator snared to the radiator to ensure than the enclosure can't get excessively hot. A few guardians like to have alerts that report when temperatures are above or beneath the focused on temperature ranges. There are economical laser-guided handheld thermometers promptly accessible that permits quick spot-checking of the temperatures in various regions of the fenced in area. We suggest anybody with a pet turtle have one since it permits you to know the temperature variety all through the walled in area. You can even place the laser dab onto the carapace of the turtle to see check how warm it is. Try not to put the laser spot close to the head since it can cause perpetual harm and visual deficiency in the event that it strikes an eye.

There are many arranged eating regimens accessible for turtles. Most are terrible for Russian turtles yet there are a couple of worthy ones. Don't hesitate to converse with us about our present proposals.

With a fitting lavishly planted walled in area, wealthy in grasses and little "weeds, for example, spurges, there is little need to offer supplemental food, for example, produce. Regardless, a serving of mixed greens blend is frequently valued by open air turtles and protects that the turtles are getting enough to eat. The fundamental serving of mixed greens blend for Russian turtles kept up in outside very much planted walled in areas incorporates an assortment of greens: romaine lettuce, green or red leaf lettuce, escarole, kale, collard greens, mustard greens, turnip greens, spinach, broccoli, and other dull green verdant vegetables. We suggest blending the produce blend in with Oxbow Hay's Salad Style Grass Hay Blend to build the fiber content. Numerous Russian turtles figure out how to eat Zoo Med's Grassland Forest Diet, by and large after it has been absorbed water for 10-15 minutes, and this additionally is useful to keep up adequate fiber in the eating routine. Littler Russian turtles regularly need every day plates of mixed greens while grown-ups by and large excel on three servings of mixed greens seven days, notwithstanding their day by day touching.

Indoor turtles may get a comparable blend, yet include some new plant material, for example, new grass cuttings, minuscule weeds, hibiscus or mulberry leaves, and thorny pear desert flora cushions or thorny pear organic products. Over-taking care of produce, or offering produce that is high in basic sugars and dampness, for example, bananas and apples, may prompt looseness of the bowels.

Sprinkling a limited quantity of calcium, for example, calcium carbonate, calcium lactate, or calcium citrate, onto the serving of mixed greens will help balance out the mineral substance of the food. One TUMS Ultra Antacid gives 1000 mg calcium carbonate in every tablet and 1 and 1/4 tablet is adequate calcium to enhance around 8 cups of produce. An ordinary quality TUMS gives 200 mg calcium carbonate and might be ground into a powder and blended in with around 2/3 cup of produce. This calcium supplement is generally significant for youthful developing turtles to forestall "delicate shell" (nourishing auxiliary hyperparathyroidism). On the off chance that a solid grown-up turtle approaches soil, it appears to not require minor elements added to the produce. Something else, Miner all is a decent enhancement to add to plates of mixed greens once per week. Supplementation with a trustworthy multivitamin once seven days might be advantageous, especially to infant turtles. (Be certain the nutrient is new—most powdered nutrients lose their strength inside a half

year of tearing open the seal, and they
lose it all the more rapidly whenever
presented to moistness and temperatures
above 78°F for any timeframe.

Before you sleep your turtle, it is
imperative to have us analyze it to ensure
it is sufficiently sound to persevere
through this unpleasant action!

Hibernation is essential for the normal
cycle a Russian turtle encounters in
nature. As the day length abbreviates and
cooler climate starts in the fall, Russian
turtles quit taking care of and search out
havens (hibernacula) to shield them
from the harshest winter chill. Since a
Russian turtle can't create its own body

heat, when the temperature around them falls, their digestion eases back. Taking care of quits during hibernation on the grounds that the turtle is done utilizing a similar measure of vitality as it does during warm climate. A turtle will regularly rise up out of its tunnel on bright winter days to luxuriate quickly, and may even drink water on the off chance that it is accessible, possibly to resign somewhere down in its sanctuary if sky turns cloudy and the temperature falls.

A turtle must be sound, very much fed, and all around hydrated to endure the afflictions of hibernation. It likewise should pick a tunnel or other safe house that stay above freezing. On the off chance that a turtle needs adequate muscle versus fat to last through hibernation, it might kick the bucket during this time or may develop in the spring so incapacitated it can't recover its wellbeing. In the event that the hibernaculum gets excessively chilly, the turtle will stick to death. At times, the turtle will endure brief presentation to frigid temperatures however become dazzle or create coordination issues. This spells demise for a wild turtle yet hostage turtles can be thought about with these conditions.

Hibernation prompts the Russian turtle's regenerative inclinations. Hostage female turtles that are kept inside may not deliver eggs that year and male turtles may show no tendency to court and mate. It likewise creates the impression that hibernation is essential to keep up a turtle's general wellbeing for hostage turtles that are shielded from sleeping more than quite a long while will in general have shorter life expectancies than ones that do rest normally.

Hostage turtles may rest either in a fitting outside hibernaculum, for example, an appropriately developed counterfeit tunnel, or in protected boxes kept in a cool room of the house where the temperature remains somewhere in the range of 40 and 60°F. In the event that the temperature is much above 60F, the turtle might be dynamic and go through its vitality stores excessively fast.

On the off chance that the temperature is a lot colder, the turtle may create medical issues.

CHAPTER SIX

FURTHER FACTS ABOUT RUSSIAN TORTOISE & CONCLUSION

Before a turtle is rested, it is critical to have a wellbeing test by an educated reptile veterinarian. At any rate, the turtle ought to be gauged and its body condition evaluated. A fecal parasite test and other lab work, for example, a urinalysis, complete platelet check, and blood sciences, may recognize basic hazardous conditions. A radiograph will get in any case imperceptible bladder stones which can bargain the turtle's capacity to sleep. It is ideal to do the pre-hibernation test at any rate 4 to about a month and a half before the turtle will rest, generally in late August or early September. This permits time to address basic medical issues or to make game plans for indoor consideration for turtles with significant clinical issues. Moreover, a post-hibernation test is prescribed to decide whether the turtle has built up any issues that may require veterinary consideration.

Russian turtles likewise go through a time of rest during the most blazing driest long periods of summer known as "aestivation". In the event that the fence in area has a lot of shade and gets normally watered, a Russian turtle may stay dynamic as of now. Else it might withdraw to its tunnel and just be dynamic promptly in the first part of the day or even around evening time! Happy turtle raising!

THE END

Printed in Great Britain
by Amazon

59928473R00038